WHOLE WIDE WORLD

COLOSSEUM

by Kristine Spanier, MLIS

Ideas for Parents and Teachers

Pogo Books let children practice reading informational text while introducing them to nonfiction features such as headings, labels, sidebars, maps, and diagrams, as well as a table of contents, glossary, and index.

Carefully leveled text with a strong photo match offers early fluent readers the support they need to succeed.

Before Reading

- "Walk" through the book and point out the various nonfiction features. Ask the student what purpose each feature serves.
- Look at the glossary together. Read and discuss the words.

Read the Book

- Have the child read the book independently.
- Invite him or her to list questions that arise from reading.

After Reading

- Discuss the child's questions. Talk about how he or she might find answers to those questions.
- Prompt the child to think more. Ask: What did you know about the Colosseum before reading this book? What more would you like to learn about it?

Pogo Books are published by Jump!
5357 Penn Avenue South
Minneapolis, MN 55419
www.jumplibrary.com

Library of Congress Cataloging-in-Publication Data

Names: Spanier, Kristine, author.
Title: Colosseum / by Kristine Spanier.
Description: Minneapolis, Minnesota: Jump!, Inc., [2021]
Series: Whole wide world
Includes index. | Audience: Ages 7-10
Identifiers: LCCN 2020025833 (print)
LCCN 2020025834 (ebook)
ISBN 9781645277293 (hardcover)
ISBN 9781645277347 (paperback)
ISBN 9781645277309 (ebook)
Subjects: LCSH: Colosseum (Rome, Italy)–Juvenile literature.
Amphitheaters–Rome–Juvenile literature.
Rome (Italy)–Buildings, structures, etc.–Juvenile literature.
Architecture, Roman–Italy–Rome–Juvenile literature.
Classification: LCC DG68.1 .S65 2021 (print)
LCC DG68.1 (ebook) | DDC 937/.63–dc23
LC record available at https://lccn.loc.gov/2020025833
LC ebook record available at https://lccn.loc.gov/2020025834

Editor: Jenna Gleisner
Designer: Molly Ballanger

Photo Credits: David Wayne Buck/Shutterstock, cover; Krikkiat/Shutterstock, 1; A StockStudio/Shutterstock, 3; North Wind Picture Archives/Alamy, 4; FALKENSTEINFOTO/Alamy, 5; Francesco Todaro/Shutterstock, 6-7; Michael Nicholson/Getty, 8; Keith Lance/Getty, 8-9; James.Pintar/Shutterstock, 10; Universal Images Group/SuperStock, 11; Evgenii Iaroshevskii/Shutterstock, 12-13; Luckyphotographer/Dreamstime, 14-15; OlegAlbinsky/iStock, 16; Vladislav Gajic/Shutterstock, 17; metha1819/Shutterstock, 18-19; Martina Badini/Shutterstock, 20-21; SAHACHATZ/Shutterstock, 23.

Printed in the United States of America at Corporate Graphics in North Mankato, Minnesota.

TABLE OF CONTENTS

CHAPTER 1

GLADIATOR BATTLES

A lion is released from a trapdoor. A **gladiator** is ready to fight! The two face off. The crowd cheers. Welcome to the Colosseum!

Gladiators fought one another in this **stadium**. They also fought animals such as lions, tigers, and bears. The people of **ancient** Rome came to watch!

Construction began almost 2,000 years ago. Emperor Vespasian wanted a gathering place. The stadium opened in 80 CE. It is 164 feet (50 meters) tall.

WHAT DO YOU THINK?

The Colosseum was a gathering place for the people of Rome. Where do people gather in your community?

Plays were performed here. So were **mock** sea battles. How? The arena was flooded with water. People also loved to watch chariot races!

chariot race

CHAPTER 2

BUILT FOR THE PEOPLE

The stadium had 80 entrances. They were numbered. Tickets showed which one to use. People had assigned areas to sit in.

More than 50,000 people could fit inside. It only took 15 minutes to fill or empty the stadium! Passages helped them move quickly.

seats

Action took place in the center. Seats wrapped all the way around. This makes it an **amphitheater**. It is still the largest one on Earth!

A large **awning** could cover the top. Why? This protected **spectators** from rain or sun. Hundreds of people moved it into place.

WHAT DO YOU THINK?

Stadiums today are designed like the Colosseum. Have you been to a stadium? Did you have a good view of the action?

The Colosseum was made of rock and concrete. **Terraces** were made of marble. Clay tiles covered the floor.

TAKE A LOOK!

There are three levels. A different kind of column was used for each one. Take a look!

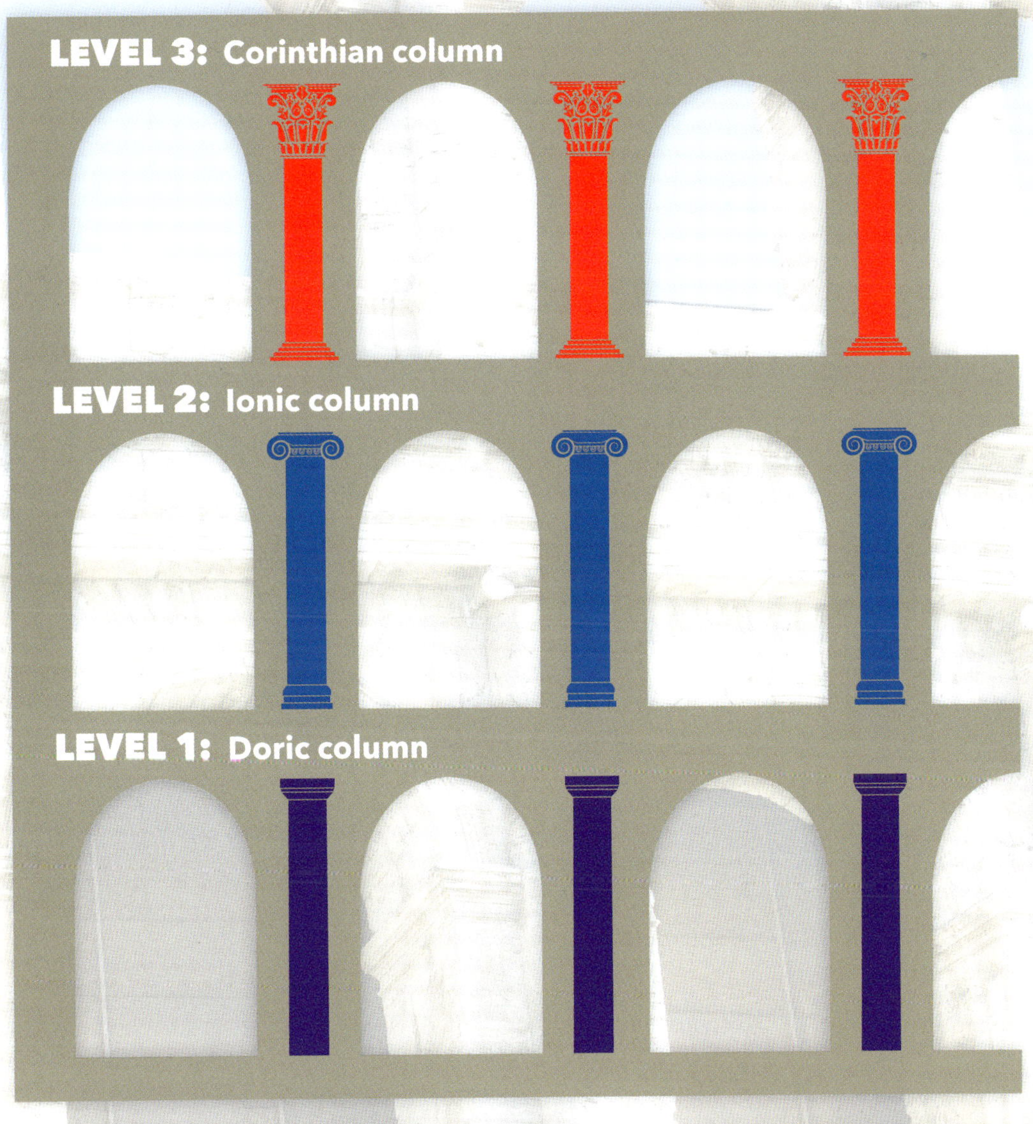

CHAPTER 3

A SYMBOL OF ITALY

People grew unhappy with the violent battles. Valentinian III **banned** them in 438 CE. Marble seats were removed from the **structure**. Statues were melted. Some materials were used to build St. Peter's Basilica in Rome.

A great **earthquake** shook it in 1231 CE. One side collapsed. Lightning has also damaged it.

Much work has been done to **restore** it. Dirt has been cleaned off the outside. Gates have been put back in place. A new floor is in the arena. People can see where gladiators waited below.

DID YOU KNOW?

A **colossal** statue of Emperor Nero once stood nearby. It was at least 100 feet (30 m) tall. It was so big that some say it gave the Colosseum its name. No one knows what happened to it.

new floor

The Colosseum is a **symbol** of Rome's history. Special events take place here again. People watch concerts. They see fireworks. More people visit it than any other **monument** in Italy! Would you like to visit?

WHAT DO YOU THINK?

The building is on the five euro cent coin. What images have you seen on coins? Why do you think they were chosen?

QUICK FACTS & TOOLS

AT A GLANCE

COLOSSEUM

Location: Rome, Italy

Size: 620 by 513 feet (189 by 156 m), 164 feet (50 m) tall

Year Construction Began: Between 70 and 72 CE

Year Open: 80 CE

Past Use: stadium for events

Current Use: monument and special event venue

Number of Visitors Each Year: around 7 million

GLOSSARY

amphitheater: A large building or area with rows of seats in a high circle around a central place such as a stage.

ancient: Belonging to a period long ago.

awning: A piece of cloth, metal, or wood that is fastened to the top of a window or to the front roof of a building to shade it from sun and help keep out rain.

banned: Officially forbade something or prevented someone from doing something.

colossal: Very large or huge.

earthquake: A sudden, violent shaking of Earth that may damage buildings and cause injuries.

gladiator: A person in ancient Rome who fought other people or wild animals, often to the death, in order to provide entertainment.

mock: Imitation or not real.

monument: A statue, building, or other structure that reminds people of an event or a person.

restore: To bring back to an original condition.

spectators: People who watch an event but do not participate in it.

stadium: A large structure in which sporting events and concerts are held.

structure: Something that has been built.

symbol: An object that stands for, suggests, or represents something else.

terraces: Balconies of a building.

INDEX

TO LEARN MORE

Finding more information is as easy as 1, 2, 3.

1. Go to www.factsurfer.com
2. Enter "Colosseum" into the search box.
3. Choose your book to see a list of websites.